food
technology
TEACHER'S GUIDE

Steve Cushing

Contents

Introduction

About this Teacher's Guide

Lesson plans and worksheets

This Teacher's Guide has been written to support the Design in the Making: Food Technology Pupil's Book. All of the material provided in both this guide and the Pupil's Book has been successfully used in schools with students. Alongside a number of lesson plans this guide contains a large number of photocopiable worksheets. This will enable you, the teacher, to focus on carrying out practical activities with students. Whilst you may not wish to use all of the worksheets provided, many of them will help you to provide the necessary structure to create a quality teaching and learning environment in your food technology area. The optional lesson plans provided in this guide have been written with Year 7 and 8 in mind. The tasks outlined for Year 9 provide one single overarching activity relating to biscuits. This is to prepare students for the type of work that they will need to undertake if they choose GCSE food technology courses. For this reason one single 'scheme of work plan' is provided. The plans are cross-referenced to sections of the Pupil's Book and to the National Curriculum Statutory Programmes of Study. Taken together, the lesson plans provide opportunities to cover all areas of the National Curriculum that are relevant to Food Technology.

Homework

Care has been taken to ensure that students do not need copies of the Pupil's Book at home to complete the homework outlined in the lesson plans.

Flexibility

The materials in this guide and in the Pupil's Book do not aim to prescribe a single way to teach food technology. The author recognises that teachers need to use their own expertise and enthusiasm to create an exciting and practical experience for students. Although the photocopiable worksheets support activities in the Pupil's Book, and the book has been written in a sequence, the author anticipates the material being used in a wide variety of ways. Students should be able to dip into the textbook to support their learning at various times.

The Pupil's Book can be used when the teacher is absent, if necessary. There are a number of activities in the book that can be completed using pencil and paper. Although practical activity is recommended throughout the text, the Pupil's Book also aims to support the theoretical knowledge that underpins this practical activity.

Information about the Pupil's Book

Gaining the skills necessary to create interesting and exciting things to eat, alongside an understanding of the importance of healthy eating, is a valuable lesson we all need to learn. Design in the Making takes the view that food technology is about developing ideas for things to make with food ingredients and having the knowledge, skills and understanding to realise these ideas. Food technology is a practical subject, and should be fun. It is by making things that students gain many of the skills that they need to design and make or modify food products. But it is also important that they have a grasp of the theoretical knowledge which underpins any food technology activity.

The Pupil's Book contains some of the theoretical knowledge that students will need to be able to design and make quality products using food. This Teacher's Guide provides structure and helpful sheets to enable you to make full use of the Pupil's Book. Although the Pupil's Book contains suggestions for practical tasks, you will need to guide your students and tell them which sections of the book they should be working from.

The Pupil's Book contains a number of basic recipes to help them learn how to combine and process foods in a variety of ways. Although the book has been developed for Key Stage 3, with the knowledge and skills it contains it will also be an extremely useful resource for students undertaking GCSE courses at Key Stage 4.

Designing and making

Designing cannot be separated from making. They form a single integrated activity. This means that when students are designing they should be thinking about how their products could be made, and when they are making food items they should be thinking about how the product can be better designed.

Knowledge and skills
It is not possible for anyone to design anything without some practical knowledge of materials and the making skills needed to turn materials into something useful. Students should not see designing as something they do prior to making and then forget about. When making food products, they should also be thinking about changes that can be made to improve their product and how they would modify their recipe if they made the food product again.

Practical activities
Through practical activities you will need to ensure that students learn the skills needed to produce good quality food outcomes. This may include product disassembly – looking at existing products to see what they are made of. A simple way of doing this is to look at product labels. The Pupil's Book and Teacher's Guide contain a number of labels, so that there is no need to visit the supermarket. Some practical activities are aimed at giving students an opportunity to practise new skills, concepts and procedures. Other activities will enable them to put their knowledge, skills and understanding to effective use. The best way to learn is to put knowledge and skills to the test.

Using ICT
Wherever possible students should use ICT to enhance their design and technology work. The Pupil's Book does not refer to ICT use, as some schools do not have extensive access to ICT equipment. Given this situation, there are no activities that rely solely upon such access. Guidance is given in the Teacher's Guide on activities which *can* be combined with ICT. Teachers should make use of new technologies wherever they can enhance student learning. This could be by using dietary analysis tables. Students can also use ICT to enhance the quality of their work.

The Internet
The Internet provides a valuable source of information relating to design and technology in food. Some information on useful sites is provided in this Teacher's Guide.

Starting to use the Teacher's Guide

The first lesson plan is designed as an introduction for teachers and will enable them to become familiar with the format used. The first two worksheets correspond to this lesson plan and perform a similar function for students.

Preparing for OFSTED

What inspectors are looking for when judging your lessons

Teaching

Your knowledge and understanding of the subject you are teaching. How the lesson links/builds upon earlier lessons. How clear the lesson aims and objectives are. Your expectation of your pupils. Your use of Q and A; vocabulary; insistence on accuracy. The effectiveness of your department and lesson planning. Appropriateness and variety of activities and tasks to suit the curricular objectives and needs of your pupils. Your control and organisation of the class. Have you differentiated the lesson effectively – EO and SEN? Your use of the school's resources and effective use of time available – pace of lesson, does it finish on time? Contribution the lesson and your teaching make to SMSC. Do you give equal attention to pupils of both sexes and all abilities, including SEN? Thoroughness of your marking and assessment. Do you assess pupils' work effectively and use assessment to inform your teaching? Do you use homework to reinforce and extend learning, not simply to enable pupils to finish off work?

Response of pupils to the lesson

What are your pupils' attitudes, behaviour and motivation like? Are the pupils keen to participate or bored? Relationship between pupil and you; between pupils themselves, including racial harmony. Do pupils/you respect the feelings and values of others? Do pupils work together well? Pupil ability to concentrate, their capacity for personal study and ability to solve problems. Selection of resources by pupils – do they show initiative and acceptance of responsibility? Do pupils show ability to persevere with difficult tasks?

Attainment

How far the attainment of pupils matches national standards: KS3 – should achieve NC level 5/6 by the end of KS; KS4 – should achieve GCSE C grade by the end of KS; A Level – should achieve grade C/E by end of course. An assessment is made upon what pupils know, understand and can do. Are there any significant variations in attainment – gender, ethnicity, background? What do your records and pupils' records show? What are the pupils' oral and written attainments? How does this relate to SEN pupils – IEPs, prior attainment and targets. Evidence is gained from lesson and discussion with pupils.

Progress

How effective is the lesson in consolidating knowledge, skills and understanding; is the rate of progress appropriate for this level of attainment? Are there any specific elements of progress; variations between boys and girls? Where is new knowledge gained, skills acquired and understanding extended? Amount learnt or consolidated in lesson. Does the lesson offer sufficient challenge to pupils?

Other significant evidence

Competence in applying reading, writing, speaking, listening and numeracy skills. Aspects of planning, resources, accommodation which have impacts on standards or quality. Marking of books, quality of worksheets, textbooks. Spacing of lessons through cycle. Use of support staff.

Level Descriptions

Level	Designing	Achieved	Making	Achieved
L3	I have drawn and labelled a number of ideas.		I have accurately measured and mixed together ingredients	
	My ideas fulfil parts of the brief		I have decorated my finished dish	
	I have described how I intend to make my ideas, including which equipment and ingredients I will need			
	I have suggested some other ideas after starting to plan my work			
	I have evaluated my work and suggested changes where they are necessary			
	I have used information from my notes to design my solution			
L4	I have collected information together to help in developing my ideas, this information takes into account the views of the people who will use my solution		I have accurately measured, weighed and combined a number of ingredients in different ways to make my solution	
	I have drawn and labelled a number of different ideas and described why some are better solutions than others		I have carefully presented my dish, displaying it to good effect	
	I have produced a step by step plan of how I intend to make my solution, listing all of the equipment and ingredients I will need			
	I have evaluated my work as I do it, suggesting improvements and developments which would improve the end product			
L5	I have collected information from a number of places, including looking at products which are similar to my ideas		I have used a range of equipment and ingredients safely, accurately and hygienically	
	I have discussed and sketched my ideas and plans		I have used and recorded checking procedures as I made my solution	
	My plans have altered as I have spotted possible difficulties			
	I have used my plans as I made my solution			
	I have evaluated my work as it progressed, commenting on how my solution will be used and how it is limited due to the available ingredients			
	I have compared my solution to the original design brief and suggested how it could be developed further			

Level	Designing	Achieved	Making	Achieved
L6	I have carried out research into a number of areas, including looking at similar products and those that may influence my ideas		I have used a range of equipment, ingredients and techniques to a high standard, my solution is well made and well presented, it works well	
	I have planned my work carefully, taking into account appearance, function, safety and who will use the final solution, I have used this information to develop a design proposal			
	I have tried out parts of my solution to help with planning my final idea			
	I have included in my plan ways of proceeding if something goes wrong			
	I have evaluated my solution in use, carrying out tests and seeking the opinions of others and suggested improvements that could be made			
L7	I have collected together a range of research materials which I have used to develop my ideas		I have carried out tests on similar products to influence my choice of ingredients, processes and the final form of my solution	
	I have taken into account the influence of the predicted users of my solution			
	I have developed ways of testing my solution which will best investigate whether it fulfils the original design brief and ways to develop further ideas		I have taken into account the effects that combining certain ingredients and using certain processes can have on the final outcome	
	I have used a variety of different ways to describe my intentions to others, including the presentation of my solution			
	My plans include equipment, processes, ingredients and how long each operation will take			
	I have recorded, with clear reasons, how and why my ideas have had to change as circumstances have changed during making			

National Curriculum Coverage

Lesson	National Curriculum Units	Making	Designing
1 Teaching design skills	1a, 2a, 2b	4b, 4f, 8b, 8d, 9b, 9d	1a, 1b, 1e, 1i, 1j, 1l
2 Technological changes	1a, 2a, 2b	4b, 5b, 6c, 8a, 8c, 8d, 9b, 10a, 10b, 10c	3i
3 Using recipes	1a, 1b, 1c, 2a, 2b	4b, 4c, 4i, 8a, 8b, 8c	3f, 3g, 3i
4 Making and evaluating a food product	1a, 1b, 2a, 2b	4c, 4j, 8b, 8c, 8d, 10a, 10b, 10c	3f, 3g, 3k, 3l
5 Flavouring food	1a, 1b, 2a, 2b	4d, 4j, 5b, 5c, 8a, 8b, 8c, 10a, 10b, 10c	1a, 3e, 3g, 3k, 3l
6 Practical investigations into staple foods	1a, 2a, 2b	4b, 4i, 5c, 8b, 8c, 8d, 10a, 10b, 10c	3a, 3b, 3f, 3g, 3h, 3k, 3l
7 A staple food recipe	1a, 2a, 2b	4b, 4f, 4j, 5c, 8b, 8c, 8d, 10a, 10b, 10c	3e, 3f, 3g, 3h, 3k, 3l
8 Convenience foods	1a, 1b, 1c, 2a, 2b	5a, 5b, 8a, 8b, 8f, 9a, 10a, 10c	
9 Electrical equipment	1a, 1b, 1c, 2a, 2b	4b, 4e, 5a, 5c, 6c, 8c, 9b, 10a, 10b, 10c	3g, 3i
10 Lunch time snack 1	1a, 2a, 2b	4b, 4f, 4i, 4j, 4k, 5a, 5c, 8b, 8c, 8d, 9a, 10a, 10b, 10c	3a, 3b, 3c, 3d, 3e, 3g, 3h, 3k, 3l
11 Lunch time snack 2	1a, 2a, 2b	4b, 4f, 4j, 4k, 5a, 5c, 8b, 8c, 8d, 9a, 10a, 10b, 10c	3e, 3g, 3h, 3k, 3l
12 Packaging a food product	1a, 1c, 2a, 2b	4g, 5a, 7a, 7c, 7d, 8b, 8c, 8d, 9c, 9d	3a, 3b, 3d, 3f, 3g, 3j, 3l
13 Biscuit project 1	1a, 1c	5c	3a, 3b, 3c, 3d, 3e, 3f, 3g, 8a, 8b, 8c, 8d, 8e, 8f
14 Biscuit project 2	1a, 1c, 2a, 2b	4a, 4b, 4g, 4h, 4i, 4j, 4k, 5a, 5b, 5c, 5d, 10a, 10b, 10c	3h, 3i, 3j, 3k, 3l, 8a, 8b, 8c, 8d, 8f
15 Biscuit project 3	1a, 1c, 2a, 2b	4d, 4g, 4h, 4i, 4j, 4k, 5a, 5b, 5c, 5d, 5e, 10a, 10b, 10c	8a, 8b, 8c
16 Biscuit project 4	1a, 1c, 2a, 2b	4c, 4d, 4h, 4k, 6e, 10a, 10b, 10c	3f, 3h, 3i, 8e, 9a, 9b, 9c, 9d

Mark Sheet and Pupil's Record

Quality Control   Staff name _____

Name of dish _____

Date of Practical _____

Checklist	Attainment	Student name							
Personal Hygiene	Excellent								
	Good								
	Satisfactory								
	Unsatisfactory								
Food Preparation	Excellent								
	Good								
	Satisfactory								
	Unsatisfactory								
Cook Food Thoroughly	Excellent								
	Good								
	Satisfactory								
	Unsatisfactory								
Clean Environment	Excellent								
	Good								
	Satisfactory								
	Unsatisfactory								
Clean Equipment	Excellent								
	Good								
	Satisfactory								
	Unsatisfactory								
Product Quality	Excellent								
	Good								
	Satisfactory								
	Unsatisfactory								

Pupil's Record of Competence

As you work through the activities, you will acquire many new skills and with practice become competent at working in the food environment. Each time you practise a new skill, record what you have achieved. At the end of each stage your teacher should sign your record.

Date	Skill	Use of Equipment	Notes

Teacher's signature: _____ Date: _____

Teaching Design Skills

Introducing design skills

Before pupils can fully utilise their skills and knowledge to solve practical problems, they need to understand the principles behind the processes involved in designing. Good design does not take place in a vacuum.

A fun way to introduce design problem-solving is shown on Worksheet 1. Pupils are asked to draw simple line drawings on the worksheet to show how the two people shown could cross the river. There are literally hundreds of ways, including obvious ways such as swimming, building a bridge, boat or tunnel, and more outrageous ways like drinking the water, being fired out of a cannon or walking around the river's source.

Once the pupils have drawn their methods, the teacher should first focus upon understanding the problem in more detail. It is highly unlikely that any of the pupils will have asked for clarification of the problem. For example:
- How deep or wide is the river?
- How fast does it flow?
- Are there dangerous creatures living in it?
- How much time do I have to get across?

Whilst they will not ask these questions, the solution to the design problem will be very dependent upon such factors. Why build a boat if the river is 4 centimetres deep?

Having established the need for clear details relating to the design problem to be solved, the next step is to consider other important factors. To build a boat you would need both the skills and knowledge and the right materials to be available in the correct quantities.

Constraints

Design is about fully understanding a problem, relating individual and group skills, knowledge and expertise, including awareness of constraints, and thus reaching an optimum and cost effective solution. By changing the constraints, you, the teacher can make a problem easier or more difficult. This enables differentiation by task. For example, if you had given out the river crossing worksheet to three groups of pupils, grouped by ability:
- One group could be asked to complete the task as specified with no design constraints.
- A second group might be asked to complete the task but with the knowledge that the river is one mile wide, 10 metres deep and contains alligators.
- A third group could be given these constraints plus 35 minutes to cross the river.

The more constraints that need to be considered, the more difficult the task becomes.

Lesson Plan 1   Teaching design skills

Type

Designing

Support material

Worksheet 1 (How would you get to the other side of a river?), Worksheet 2 (Ideas for crossing a river) and Worksheet 3 (A guide to problem solving).

Knowledge (Pupil's Book)

Pupil's Book pages 4–5.

Aim of lesson

To teach the concept of design.

Before

Introduction to food technology and the design process.

At the end pupils should be able to:

- Analyse a problem, fully exploring factors such as skills, knowledge of materials and constraints.
- Understand that constraints in problem-solving increase the difficulty of the task.

Next

Skills-based focused activities, to relate problem-solving to food technology.

Brief description

Pupils will be asked to design different ways of crossing a river, then to look at problem specification and the importance of skills and resources.

Differentiation

Mainly by outcome, but you may wish to increase the number of constraints and potential solutions for more able pupils.

Assessment

A – Pupils produce a well-illustrated and annotated diagram with at least twenty-five solutions.
B – Pupils produce a well-illustrated diagram, but limited and unimaginative solutions.
C – Pupils are capable of teacher directed solutions.

Homework

Pupils could be given a number of similar design activities based in a kitchen environment, e.g. how to prevent hazards in the kitchen – seen and unseen.

Resources

- Drawing equipment.

Teaching tips

- Enthuser, sounding board for pupil ideas.
- Facilitator, needed to keep pupils on track and lesson moving at a rapid pace.

Lesson Plan 2 Technological changes

Type

Knowledge-based

Support material

Worksheet 4a (How things have changed in the kitchen 1), Worksheet 4b (How things have changed in the kitchen 2), Worksheet 5 (Hygiene quiz), Worksheet 6 (Hygiene quiz – clues sheet) and Worksheet 7 (Be a bug buster!).

Knowledge (Pupil's Book)

Pupil's Book pages 9–10 (Health, safety and hygiene).

Aim of lesson

To present a historical perspective of the origins of food technology.

Before

Introduction to food technology. Provide a definition of the subject and what pupils will be taught and what you expect them to learn.

At the end pupils should be able to:

- Give a detailed account of the technological changes that have occurred in the kitchen environment. (Emphasis should be placed on the storage, preparation and cooking of food in relation to the importance of hygiene.)

Next

An introduction to basic food hygiene and – in preparation for making activities with food – a guide to avoiding food poisoning.

Brief description

Using information from the Pupil's Book, introduce the topic to pupils. Pupils will form small groups to discuss the technological changes and record their observations. You will lead a class discussion to consolidate the lesson. You could ask pupils to present their findings and debate the issue 'Is today's kitchen healthier, safer and cleaner than before?' A class display 'Then and Now' could be produced.

Differentiation

By outcome, based on knowledge. Less able pupils will be able to identify key concepts and words. Their work should show that technological changes have taken place over time. More able pupils should be able to transfer knowledge and understanding from other subject areas and give reasons for the technological changes and relate them to other historical events, e.g. Industrial Revolution.

Assessment

A – Pupils show a clear understanding of history and how technological changes have enhanced the kitchen environment and improved the quality of food we eat.
B – Pupils have an understanding of the changes that have occurred and why they are important.
C – Pupils can describe and compare the historical changes.

Homework

Activity 5 (page 9) – The importance of personal hygiene.
Activity 6 (page 10) – Design a poster that promotes the importance of hygiene in your technology classroom.

Resources

• The poster could be designed on computer.

Teaching tips

• You will need to structure pupil discussion and consolidate their knowledge and understanding.

Lesson Plan 3 Using recipes

Type

Practical skills-based

Support material

Worksheet 8 (Chocolate chip cookie recipes), Worksheet 9 (Chocolate chip cookies – healthy or not?), Worksheet 10 (Break down a recipe), Worksheet 11 (Identifying hand equipment), Worksheet 12 (Identifying electrical equipment), Worksheet 13 (Weight and measure – the secret of success), Worksheet 14 (Cooking and heat transfer), Worksheet 15 (Costing recipes) and Worksheet 16 (Staple foods practical diary).

Knowledge (Pupil's Book)

Pupil's Book pages 9–10 (Health, safety and hygiene) and page 11 (Using recipes).

Aim of lesson

To raise pupils awareness of the need to interpret and understand recipes if they are to develop the necessary making skills to produce a successful, quality food item that is safe to eat.

Before

Introduction to food hygiene.

At the end the pupils should be able to:

- Understand the structure of a recipe.
- Recognise the importance of the content.
- Identify the need to disassemble a recipe carefully before embarking on making the product to ensure a successful outcome.

Next

Making an edible food item in a hygienic environment.

Brief description

As a class discussion, and introduction to recipes, pupils will disassemble the chocolate chip cookies recipe. They will investigate proportions of ingredients and practise weighing and measuring skills, with a focus on accuracy. Pupils will produce a detailed making plan to ensure they are organised and prepared to make the biscuits.

Differentiation

Less able pupils should be able to weigh and measure accurately and follow a given recipe. More able pupils should be able to draw on their experience and mathematical understanding to help them consider keeping the right proportions when modifying ingredients and creating their own recipes.

Assessment

A – Pupils should present a clear, logical plan of how to make the biscuits. The plan should identify specialist knowledge about the function of each ingredient, the skilful use of each piece of equipment and an understanding of technical terms to avoid problems during making.

B – Pupils should give a clear, logical plan of how to make the biscuits and the tools needed.

C – With help, they can understand a basic plan of how to make the biscuits.

Homework

Activity 16 (Pupil's Book page 18) – Using information gathered from the local supermarket, work out the cost of the biscuits.

Resources

• Enlarged (A3) version of the chocolate chip cookie recipe to use as a focal point on the board.

Teaching tips

• The first practical activity could be noisy – inform and educate pupils
• Individual support to pupils as necessary.
• Ensure a safe working environment whilst supervising activities.

Lesson Plan 4

Making and evaluating a food product

Type

Making activity

Support material

Worksheet 9 (Chocolate chip cookies – healthy or not?)

Knowledge (Pupil's Book)

Pupil's Book pages 14–15 (Understanding heat).

Aim of lesson

For every pupil to produce a batch of chocolate chip cookies in a safe and hygienic environment and achieve a certificate of competence at the end.

Before

Recipe disassembly and careful planning.

At the end pupils should be able to:

- Use basic hand tools safely and appropriately.
- Switch on and use the cooker safely.
- Demonstrate a high standard of personal hygiene.
- Demonstrate a high degree of practical competence.
- Produce a successful batch of edible biscuits.

Next

Following on from the homework activity, a more detailed look at basic nutrition as an introduction to staple foods as part of a healthy, balanced diet.

Brief description

You will give a brief practical demonstration (no more than 10 minutes).
Pupils will be supervised while they make the biscuits. There will be a class discussion to compare results and evaluate the quality of each biscuit.

Differentiation

Less able pupils should use the simplified, modified recipe to make the biscuits. More able pupils should anticipate problems in the making process (i.e. understand the need to obtain the right consistency of dough), and should suggest sensible solutions to the problems in the specialist knowledge column of the time plan.

Assessment

- Fill in practical mark sheet (page 9).
- Award certificates of competence, if appropriate, to individual pupils.

Homework

Complete Worksheet 9 (Chocolate chip cookies – healthy or not?).

Resources

Chocolate chip cookie ingredients and utensils.

Teaching tips

- Practical demonstration (hint: first practical and therefore could be noisy).
- Ensure a safe environment is maintained.
- Ensure adequate pace to the lesson so that the product is completed within available time.

Lesson Plan 5   Flavouring food

Type

Design and make focused task

Support material

Worksheet 16 (Staple foods practical diary]

Knowledge (Pupil's Book)

Pupil's Book pages 25–26 (Definition of flavour), page 30 (Adding flavour to foods) and pages 14–15 (Understanding heat).

Aim of lesson

To explore ways of flavouring food using herbs, spices and aromatic seeds.

Before

Work on hygiene and on safe use of equipment, e.g. oven.

At the end pupils should be able to:

- Use flavourings to enhance their food products.
- Produce an omelette in a safe and hygienic environment.
- Develop further practical skills, e.g. use of hob and practice of temperature control.

Next

Flavouring staple foods.

Brief description

Groups of pupils will make a simple omelette using no more than two herbs, spices or aromatic seeds. They will complete a taste test using sensory descriptors.

Differentiation

By outcome – focus should be on pupil's ability to work safely and to demonstrate confident practical skills. A degree of independence by individuals will differentiate them.

Assessment

Practical competency (see mark sheet on page 9). Working towards achieving a certificate of competence.

Homework

Activity 27 (Pupil's Book page 33).

Resources

Provide ingredients – eggs and a selection of herbs, spices and aromatic seeds.

Teaching tips

- Class demonstration.
- Individual support as necessary.
- Carefully structure the taste tests to ensure that all pupils get access to a range of flavours.
- Enthuser, encourage pupils to try unusual and unfamiliar flavours.

Lesson Plan 6

Practical investigations into staple foods

Type

Design and make

Support material

Worksheet 17 (Designing an original staple food recipe) and Worksheet 18 (Making plan)

Knowledge (Pupil's Book)

Pupil's Book pages 34–36 (Basic sauces), pages 37–38 (Recipes for Sauces), page 39 (Recipes for Pasta Dishes), pages 40–41 (Cereals) and pages 45–46 (Potato recipes).

Aim of lesson

To develop the practical capability of the pupils through making and investigating a variety of staple food recipes.

Before

An understanding of basic nutrition and structure of recipes.

At the end pupils should be able to:

- Produce a coloured diagram of their design idea, clearly labelled with the ingredients.
- Identify the staple food.
- Produce a making time plan or flowchart to show the logical steps of making.

Next

Design their own staple food recipe and then make a successful product.

Brief description

Using the recipes in the book, split the class into groups and give each group a different staple food to discuss and experiment with. Pupils will record their findings and share them with the class in a plenary session.

Differentiation

Less able pupils will need help to estimate the proportions needed for each ingredient. More able pupils should use recipes in the Pupil's Book to help generate ideas for a recipe that combines a variety of ingredients and uses of flavours effectively. They should also be able to estimate the proportions of ingredients

Assessment

A – Pupils should produce a good clear diagram with detailed annotation clearly explaining their intentions. The recipe must draw on a variety of skills and test the pupil's knowledge and understanding of the ingredients' properties.

B – Pupils should produce a good, clear, informative design idea with annotation that clearly describes their intentions, but they may need help to think about the logical sequence of making.

C – Pupils will have had to use a recipe from the book, and will have used the modified ingredients list.

Homework

Pupil's Book page 44.

Resources

Worksheet 17 to help pupils create their own recipe.

Teaching tips

- You need to facilitate and resource, but not instruct.
- Allow pupils to generate their own ideas.
- Maintain the pace of the lesson to ensure that pupils remain task-focused.
- Give individuals support as necessary.

Lesson Plan 7 — A staple food recipe

Type

Making and evaluating

Support material

Mark sheet, Worksheet 47 (Self evaluation) and certificate of competence.

Aim of lesson

To make and evaluate a designed, healthy and balanced staple food recipe.

Before

Recipe design and planning to make a food product.

At the end pupils should be able to:

- Successfully produce their own recipe idea in a safe and hygienic environment.
- Reflect on their own practical ability and evaluate their work objectively.

Next

The popularity of staple foods as part of convenience and fast food.

Brief description

Give a brief recap of how to use a cooker safely. You should demonstrate the control of temperature when cooking and show the difference between simmer and boil. Pupils will use their making plans to produce their recipe. At the end of the lesson pupils' work should be marked and the pupils should have an opportunity to see and discuss each other's work.

Differentiation

By practical outcome.

Assessment

A – The product should have at least three stages of making not using a convenience food product, e.g. sauce from a jar, and should have an original combination of carefully considered flavours.

B – Simple making, carefully produce using fresh ingredients.

C – Two stages of making and if appropriate use of convenience food.

Homework

Worksheet 47 (Self evaluation).

Resources

- Ingredients to be provided or ensure pupils bring them.
- Could use a digital camera to photograph pupils' dishes and a computer to analyse the nutritional content.

Teaching style

- Ensure a safe and hygienic working environment.
- Facilitate pupil making activity.
- Ensure pace.
- Assess practical outcomes.

Lesson Plan 8   Convenience foods

Type

Research (suitable as a cover lesson)

Support material

Worksheet 20a (Healthy eating – convenience foods 1) and Worksheet 20b (Healthy eating – convenience foods 2).

Knowledge (Pupil's Book)

Pupil's Book pages 47–49 (Eating habits) and pages 49–51 (Fast and convenience foods).

Aim of lesson

To research and assess the value of convenience and fast foods in today's society.

Before

An evaluation of the pupil's own staple food recipe and its suitability as a convenience food.

At the end pupils should be able to:

- Highlight the dietary significance of convenience and fast foods.
- Highlight the social changes that have resulted in the increased popularity of convenience and fast foods.

Next

Revision and end of section test.

Brief description

Using Worksheet 20a, pupils will assess the advantages and disadvantages of convenience foods. Arrange a class discussion to debate: 'Are convenience foods healthy or not?' Pupils will also evaluate the suitability of their own staple food product as a possible fast or convenience food.

Differentiation

Less able pupils will understand the reasons why staple foods are commonly used by manufacturers to make fast and convenience foods. More able pupils will complete Worksheet 20b.

Assessment

A – Accurately filled in the pupil worksheet with detailed and informed answers, referred to knowledge found and interpreted from the Pupil's Book.

B – Filled in pupil's worksheet with relevant and appropriate information.

C – With help, interpreted and completed pupil worksheet.

Homework

Revision for test.

Resources

- A display of fast and convenience food packaging.

Teaching tips

- Instruction and imparting knowledge to enhance understanding.

Lesson Plan 9   Electrical equipment

Type

Skills-based activity

Support material

Worksheet 24 (Sensory evaluation), mark sheet (page 9) and Worksheet 25 (Crumble evaluation).

Knowledge (Pupil's Book)

Pupil's Book pages 53–56 (Microwaves), pages 59–61 (Food processors, liquidisers and blenders), page 60 (Activity 43) and pages 72–73 (Making a crumble).

Aim of lesson

To introduce pupils to electrical equipment.

Before

Introduction to equipment and technological developments.

At the end pupils should be able to:

- Produce a food product using electrical equipment safely.
- Decide whether it is appropriate or not to use electrical equipment for a particular recipe.

Next

Use of electrical equipment, when appropriate, in future design and make activities.

Brief description

Pupils will carry out a practical investigation in groups. Organise a class discussion to feedback and discuss findings.

Differentiation

Differentiation by task and outcome. Teacher support for pupils who need it. Help given to pupils when they get into difficulty. Support from textbook and worksheets. Extend able pupils by asking for more detail and correct specialist vocabulary.

Assessment

- Assess pupils' practical competence.
- Use suggested mark sheet.

Homework

Pupil's Book page 81.

Resources

- Electric mixers.
- Food processors.
- The basic ingredients for pupils to use and taste.

Teaching tips

- Spot demonstrations.
- Ensure a safe working environment.
- Support groups of pupils as necessary.
- Ensure pace.

Lesson Plan 10   Lunch time snack 1

Type

Design activity

Support material

Worksheet 27 (Shopping survey), Worksheet 28 (Design a snack food), Worksheet 29 (Snack food recipe development – main dish), Worksheet 30 (Snack food recipe development – accompaniment), Worksheet 38 (Food product specification) and Worksheet 42 (Nutritional analysis).

Knowledge (Pupil's Book)

Pupil's Book page 64 (Nutrition and diet), pages 65–66 (Carbohydrate), pages 66–67 (Fats and Oils), pages 68–69 (Vitamins and minerals), pages 74–75 (More on minerals), pages 75–77 (More on vitamins), pages 62–63 (Soups), pages 84–85 (Dressings) and pages 88–89 (Dairy drinks).

Aim of lesson

To design a nutritious lunch time snack that is invigorating, high in fibre and low in salt, sugar and animal fat.

Before

A detailed explanation and discussion about nutrition.

At the end pupils should be able to:

- Apply their knowledge and understanding of nutrition to produce a balanced recipe.
- Use their practical experience to produce an imaginative but realistic recipe design.

Next

Make their design idea and analyse the nutritional content to test whether their idea has met the brief's requirements.

Brief description

As a class, pupils will produce a specification for the snack food. In small groups, pupils will research existing snack food products (e.g. school meals). They will generate possible ideas and assess their suitability against the specification.

Differentiation

Low ability pupils will use the recipes in the book to give them ideas: crumble (pages 72–73), salad (page 85) and milk (page 89).

More able pupils will acknowledge and accommodate special dietary requirements of others when designing.

Assessment

A – A complex recipe that is nutritionally balanced and sensitively flavoured. Pupils should be able to explain their ideas and justify their decisions for their shopping survey (Worksheet 27).

B – A realistic recipe that provides the basic nutrients and a definite flavour. Pupils should be able to explain their ideas.

C – A basic recipe design using recipes provided by you.

Homework

Healthy Eating Quiz (Activity 46 on page 69 of Pupil's Book)
Worksheet 26 (Fill your fridge)
Dear Jane (Activity 61 on page 94 of Pupil's Book)

Resources

• Access to the ideas for recipes presented in the Pupil's Book.

Teaching tips

• Differentiate, facilitate and resource pupils' design ideas.
• Provide individual support where necessary.
• Ensure pupils stay task-focused.

Lesson Plan 11   Lunch time snack 2

Type

Making activity

Support material

Worksheet 31 (Snack food evaluation).

Knowledge (Pupil's Book)

Pupil's Book pages 78–79 (More on eating habits), pages 82–85 (Salads) and pages 86–89 (Dairy products).

Aim of lesson

To make a delicious lunch time snack and analyse its nutritional content as part of a thorough evaluation.

Before

Establish an agreed specification and plan to make.

At the end pupils should be able to:

- Produce a snack food product in a safe and hygienic environment.
- Analyse the nutritional content, using a computer program if available.
- Evaluate the success of the snack food against the specification.

Next

Packaging food products. Design of packaging and food labels.

Brief description

Pupils will demonstrate their confident and competent practical skills, where appropriate, safely, using electrical as well as hand held equipment. Pupils will independently analyse the nutritional content of the product.

Differentiation

More able pupils should make a more complex and demanding food product that demonstrates the ability to organise and dovetail tasks.

Assessment

Practical mark sheet

Homework

Pupils should produce a written evaluation that describes to what degree the design idea fulfilled the specification and brief.

Teaching tips

- Facilitate practical activity.
- Ensure pace and a safe working environment.
- Provide individual support as required.
- Assess outcome.

Lesson Plan 12 — Packaging a food product

Type

Practical make activity

Support material

Worksheet 50 (Food packaging)

Knowledge (Pupil's Book)

Pupil's Book pages 90–91 (Food labels) and page 92 (Allergic reactions)

Aim of lesson

Pupils design a suitable package for their edible product. They draw the package and label the diagram with the dimensions and annotation to suggest how the package will preserve and protect the edible product.

Before

Work on fast and convenience foods, and a brief introduction to commercial, packaged foods.

At the end pupils should be able to:

• Produce a diagram of a suitable packaging idea.

Next

End of section test.

Brief description

Pupils carry out a practical investigation in groups. Organize a class discussion to feedback and talk about findings.

Differentiation

Differentiation by task and outcome. Teacher support for pupils as necessary. Ensure that all pupils are successful by supporting them with their practical work. Use textbook and worksheets to extend achievement and support learners.

Assessment

A – The package should be carefully drawn, illustrating good spatial awareness and careful use of colour and graphic design. The information on the package should be informative to the consumer.

B – The packaging design should be carefully drawn with labelling information.

C – The packaging design is simplistic.

Homework

List the information that must be put on the package to inform the customer.

Resources

- Examples of packaging to disassemble.
- Measurements, weight and nutritional analysis information of the food the pupils have made.

Teaching tips

Whole class discussion. Individual help and support as required. Keep pupils on task and maintain pace of lesson. Act as assessor and prompter throughout lesson.

Lesson Plan 13   Biscuit project 1

Type

Design and make activity (Year 9 – suitable preparation for GCSE)

Support material

Worksheet 32a (Biscuit manufacture – case study 1), Worksheet 32b (Biscuit manufacture – case study 2), Worksheet 34 (Research brainstorm), Worksheet 35 (Record of research), Worksheet 36 (Sample letter for requesting information), Worksheet 37 (Design specification) and Worksheet 38 (Food product specification).

Knowledge (Pupil's Book)

Pupil's Book page 98 (Biscuit facts), pages 102–103 (Biscuit survey information) and pages 133–135 (Designing a new food product).

Aim of lesson

To investigate and research biscuits that are available to buy.

Before

Chocolate chip cookies and design and make a snack food recipe

At the end pupils should be able to:

- Produce research into biscuits that can be bought.
- Understand what makes a successful biscuit.
- Disassemble a biscuit and identify its components and their function.

Next

Design and make their own biscuit.

Brief description

Using a variety of bought biscuits the pupils should disassemble and taste the biscuits to evaluate their success. Record their findings and present their research to the class. Produce a detailed specification to be used when designing and evaluating.

Differentiation

Less able pupils should be given worksheets for them to record their findings and to produce a specification. Organise the disassembly and taste testing with them.
More able pupils could continue the research outside school and seek out, independently, a wide variety of sources of information about biscuit manufacture.

Assessment

A – Produce a detailed investigation about bought biscuits and relate the information gathered into a thorough specification.
B – Investigate bought biscuits and produce a detailed, carefully considered specification.
C – Used the information provided to research bought biscuits and produce a specification.

Homework

Food labels (Activity 52 on page 99 of Pupil's Book)

Special arrangements

- A variety of bought biscuits.
- Computer to record and present research results.

Teaching tips

- Enthuser, instructor, facilitator.
- Ensure pace to the lesson and that all pupils are involved in generating relevant information and research from a variety of sources.

Lesson Plan 14   Biscuit project 2

Type

Design and make activity

Support material

Worksheet 41 (Recipe modification) and Worksheet 43 (Time plan).

Knowledge (Pupil's Book)

Pupil's Book pages 104–105 (Rubbing-in Method), page 107 (Sweet Biscuits), pages 118–119 (The Creaming Method), pages 120–123 (Experiments with Biscuit Ingredients) and pages 124–125 (More Biscuit Recipes).

Aim of lesson

To design an original recipe for a biscuit that can be made as a batch and has the potential to be sold in a supermarket.

Before

Detailed research and specification to constrain designs.

At the end pupils should be able to:

- Trial a variety of ways to make and flavour biscuits before deciding which design best meets their specification.
- Produce a recipe and making plan that is appropriate and workable.
- Translate the making plan into a HACCP and ensure quality when making a batch of biscuits.

Next

Make their biscuit.

Brief description

Using their specification and the variety of recipes provided in the Pupil's Book, in groups, make, test and trial different methods of making biscuits.
Using this information pupils should be able to design a biscuit recipe that is suitable and meets their specification.

Differentiation

Give worksheets to less able pupils to record their findings and produce a recipe design.
Assist with proportions, combining ingredients and a suitable method.
More able pupils should be able to work independently and use previous knowledge to make a successful and original recipe.

Assessment

A – Produce an appropriate recipe design for an original biscuit. Provide evidence to support and justify their choice of ingredients.
B – Produce a modified recipe for a biscuit.
C – Choose a recipe from the Pupil's Book to best suit pupils' tastes.

Homework

Packaging (Activities 69 and 70 on pages 128–129 of Pupil's Book).

Resources

• Buy in the basic ingredients for biscuits and a range of flavours.

Teaching tips

• Enthuser, instructor, facilitator.
• Ensure pace to the lesson and that all pupils are involved in generating relevant information. Supervise making is in a safe and hygienic environment.

Lesson Plan 15   Biscuit project 3

Type

Design and make activity

Support material

Worksheet 44 (Product evaluation).

Knowledge (Pupil's Book)

Pupil's Book page 132 (A biscuit factory).

Aim of lesson

To make a batch of biscuits using an HACCP.

Before

Recipe design and production of HACCP.

At the end pupils should be able to:

- Make a batch of biscuits in a safe and hygienic environment using labour saving devices where appropriate.
- Ensure quality control to enable them to make a batch of standard biscuits.
- Identify problems and possible solutions when making.

Next

Evaluating the biscuits' success against the specification.

Brief description

Make the biscuits using HACCP to structure the making process and ensure a quality outcome.

Differentiation

By outcome.

Assessment

A – Produce a quality batch of biscuits (i.e. they are all the same size, shape and colour) that requires more than three stages of making, dovetailing, and using labour saving equipment. Complete the practical in the time given.

B – Produce a quality batch of biscuits in the time given, using labour saving equipment.

C – Produce a batch of biscuits in the time given. Use the Teacher's Mark sheet (page 9) to assess their practical competence and standard of hygiene.

Homework

Explore batch production and produce a flowchart or storyboard.

Special arrangements

- Buy in the basic ingredients for biscuits and a range of flavours.
- Provide moulds and shapes.

Teaching tips

- Enthuser, instructor, facilitator.
- Ensure pace to the lesson and that all pupils are involved in generating relevant information. Supervise making is in a safe and hygienic environment.

Lesson Plan 16 Biscuit project 4

Type

Design and make activity

Support material

Worksheet 42 (Nutritional analysis), Worksheet 45 (Evaluation against specification) and Worksheet 44 (Product evaluation).

Knowledge (Pupil's Book)

Pupil's Book page 132 (A biscuit factory).

Aim of lesson

To evaluate the success of their biscuits against their specification and assess the suitability of their design for mass production.

Before

Make the biscuit.

At the end pupils should be able to:

- Evaluate the success of their biscuit against their specification having gathered the opinions of others.
- Assess the nutritional value of the biscuit and produce the necessary information for a packet label.
- Investigate the possibility of manufacturing their biscuit design in large quantities taking particular account of the cost.

Next

Test.

Brief description

Evaluate the success of the biscuits against the specification and assess the suitability of their design to be mass produced.

Differentiation

By outcome.

Assessment

A – Produce a detailed evaluation against their specification. This should conclude the project and explain in depth why the pupil's design is suitable or not to be mass produced.

B – Produce a detailed evaluation against their specification and suggest whether or not the pupil's design is suitable for mass production.

C – Produce an evaluation that refers to the specification and considers the possibility of mass production.

Homework

Revision for test.

Special arrangements

Computer facilities – nutritional analysis and HACCP programme and word processor and spreadsheet packages for presentation.

Teaching tips

- Consolidator and facilitator.
- Ensure pace to the lesson and that all pupils are involved in generating and recording relevant information.

Name: _____

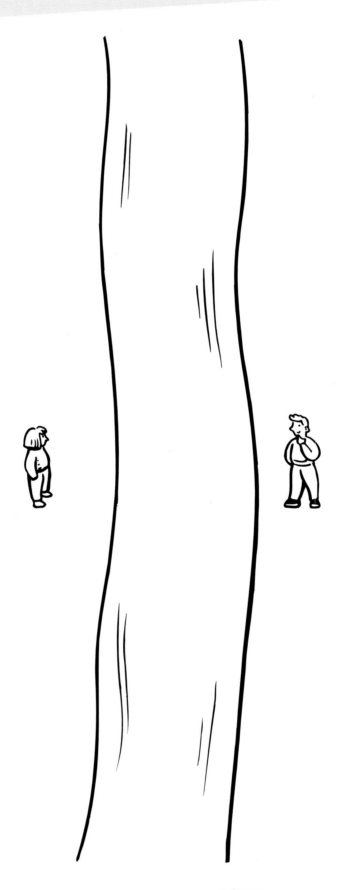

Ideas for crossing a river

Name: _____

What is a problem?

When you are given a problem to solve, what do you do? Do you have a method that you use, or do you just rush in and do the first thing which comes into your head?

If you have a method, it is easier to sort out your ideas and come to a sensible decision about what to do. People who rush straight in often find that they make the wrong sort of decision. If they do get it right, they don't know why.

Let's have a plan

The best plan is to take things slowly and in some kind of order.

Identifying the problem and generating ideas

1. First you have to think: What is the problem about? What have I got to do?
2. It's a good idea to sort out the most important things from those things that are not so important. For example, if you want to plan and prepare a meal for your family, you need to think about what they like and dislike. At school, time is important because you will have limited time for solving a problem.
3. When you have identified the important things, you can start to think about what you could make that will fit in with your ideas. You may decide immediately or have to choose from a variety of ideas.

Planning

4. Make your choice and decide what to do.
5. Check your decision. Ask other people's opinions. Make sure your idea does solve the problem!
6. Organise a plan to help you work well. Look at the recipes you are going to use. Which part of the recipe should you make first? Which part takes the longest to make? Which part takes the longest to cook, or to set? It may be that you have to start one thing, leave it while you get on with something else, and then come back to it.

Making

7. Prepare and make your meal. As you work, be aware of what you are doing. Did you get it in the right order? Did you work well and quickly? Did you allow yourself enough time? Did you take the long way round to do something, or was there a quicker way? Don't rely on your teacher to tell you how well you did or where you went wrong – tell yourself as well.

Evaluation

8. Take a good look at your results. Is there anything with which you are not happy? If you had to do the task again, is there anything you would change, and if so, how?

Name: _____

Using the pictures and information in your textbook, compare a kitchen in
the 1850s to one in use today.

1850s Kitchen	1990s Kitchen
Equipment	**Equipment**
Hygiene	**Hygiene**
Safe storage of ingredients	**Safe storage of ingredients**
Methods of cooking	**Methods of cooking**

How things have changed in the kitchen 2   W4b

Name: _____

1850s Cooking ingredients

Ingredients

How they were gathered

How they were preserved

How they were combined to make dishes to eat

1990s Cooking ingredients

Ingredients

How they are bought

How they are preserved and packaged

How they are combined to make dishes to eat

Conclusion

1. In your opinion which is the better-designed kitchen? Give reasons to justify your answer.

    _____

    _____

2. In your opinion which is the better diet? Give reasons to justify your answer.

    _____

    _____

Name: _____

Hygiene is very important, especially when preparing food.

Use the clues sheet and your textbook to help you to fill in a reason for each of these rules for good hygiene.

1. Always wash your hands after using the toilet.

    _____

2. Don't sneeze or cough on food. Use paper tissues to blow your nose on, throw them away and wash your hands afterwards.

    _____

3. Don't lick food or dip your fingers into it. Use a clean spoon to taste food.

    _____

4. Remove fancy rings and bangles before cooking. Cover cuts with a waterproof dressing.

    _____

5. Cover clothes with a clean apron or overall before working in food areas.

    _____

6. Don't brush your hair in the kitchen. Tie back long hair.

    _____

7. Prepare food on a clean work surface using clean utensils. Throw away chipped and cracked crockery.

    _____

8. Keep pets and pet food out of the kitchen.

    _____

9. Keep food covered and cool.

    _____

Name: _____

Bacteria can spread from dirty work surfaces onto food. Cracks in crockery provide a good breeding ground for bacteria.

Staphylococci bacteria on the scalp can be brushed onto food, or hair and dandruff can fall on food.

Bacteria which may grow on the skin under rings and jewellery may spread to food. Staphylococci bacteria live in cuts and sores and can easily pass onto food.

Animals can pass bacteria from their fur onto food. If pet food is left around, micro-organisms can grow on it.

Flies may land on the food and spread bacteria if it is uncovered. If food is kept cool, bacteria do not multiply so fast.

Bacteria can pass through toilet paper onto your hands and so onto food.

Staphylococci bacteria found in the nose and throat could be coughed onto food. When you blow your nose these bacteria can pass onto your hands.

Bacteria from the mouth can pass onto food from hands or spoons.

Clothing has picked up dust and dirt. Cooks in large kitchens change completely into clean clothing before preparing food.

Name: _____

Detecting whether or not harmful bacteria are present in food is not easy because bacteria are micro-organisms. This means they are too small to be seen with the human eye. To cook food safely you need to be able to prevent bacteria growing and large numbers spreading into other foods.

Answer the questions below and see if you are a Bug Buster.

2. Bacteria are living organisms. List their main needs and the most suitable conditions for them to grow and reproduce.

1. Define bacteria and name a bacteria you are familiar with. Is it harmful or not?

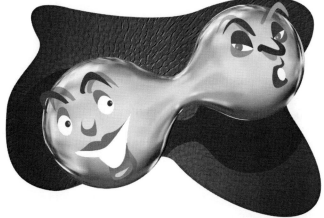

3. Identifying unseen danger! How can you identify that bacteria is present in foods?

4. The consequences! List the symptoms of food poisoning.

5. Stop the harmful bacteria from being eaten! Describe how you can test to see if your food is safe to eat.

6. Prevention is better than cure! List the important steps you must undertake to make sure you are preparing and cooking your food in a hygienic environment. Think about what you must do. How will you clean the environment? How will you stop the harmful bacteria spreading from one food to another?

Chocolate chip cookie recipes

Name: _____

Equipment
large mixing bowl
wooden and metal spoons
wire tray
baking tray
pallet knife
wooden triangle
weighing scales
oven gloves

Chocolate Chip Cookies

75 g butter
75 g brown sugar **OR** caster sugar
1 small egg
$\frac{1}{2}$ teaspoon vanilla essence
150 g self-raising flour
100 g chocolate chips **OR** chocolate drops

1 Turn the oven to Gas Mark 4 or 180 °C.

2 Grease two baking trays.

3 Cream (beat) butter and sugar in a mixing bowl with a wooden spoon until light and fluffy.

4 Beat egg, with a fork, in a small bowl. Add gradually to the creamed mixture, beating with a wooden spoon. Add vanilla essence.

5 Lightly stir in the flour using a metal spoon. Stir in the chocolate chips. **Check** the mixture for a dropping consistency. Not too runny.

6 Place heaped teaspoonfuls of the mixture on the baking tray, **leaving space** for spreading.

7 Bake in the centre of the oven for 10-15 minutes or until golden brown and firm (use oven gloves).

8 Allow to cool slightly then place on a cooling tray.

Modified Recipe

Makes 15 biscuits
Preparation time – 15 minutes
Cooking time – 15 to 20 minutes
Oven temperature – 180 °C or gas mark 4

Ingredients
75 g butter
100 g self-raising flour
50 g caster sugar
50 g milk chocolate chips

Method
Preparation
1 Set the oven to the correct temperature.
2 Lightly grease a baking tray.
3 Using a wooden spoon, cream the butter and sugar together in a large mixing bowl, until fluffy.
4 Using a metal spoon, **carefully** fold in the flour. **Do not mix or stir.** The end result should look like **breadcrumbs**, not bread dough.
5 Sprinkle in the chocolate chips and use your hands to stir them quickly into the mixture. Then use your hands to bring the mixture together into a dough. Do not play!
6 Separate the dough and make small **football** shapes. Footballs not pancakes. Space the footballs out onto the baking tray.
7 Flatten the balls slightly.
8 Using oven gloves, place the baking tray in the oven and time for 15 minues.
9 The biscuits should be taken out of the oven when they are biscuit shaped and lightly browned.

Chocolate chip cookies – healthy or not?

Name: _____

Read the information below.

Use this information to decide whether the chocolate chip cookies you made are healthy or not. Suggest changes to your recipe that will make your biscuits more healthy.

_____

_____

_____

_____

_____

Ingredients	Function	Healthy or not?
CHOCOLATE CHIPS – high in fat and sugar	Optional, but improve the taste and flavour of the biscuit.	Unhealthy: alternatives could be dried fruit or nuts, which add flavour and reduce the sugar and fat intake as well as adding more fibre.
SUGAR	Needed to cream the mixture. Sweetens the biscuit. Improves the texture, making it crumbly and crunchy.	Unhealthy: no alternative. Do not eat too often or just before bed time. Think before you eat.
MARGARINE – high in fat	Needed to cream the mixture and make a soft dough. Keeps the biscuit texture moist. Without the fat the biscuit would be dry and powdery.	Unhealthy: no alternative. Eat moderately.
FLOUR (white)	Needed the give structure to the dough and make the biscuit shape. Improves the texture, making it crumbly.	Healthy: could be improved by using brown or wholemeal flour to increase the fibre, but this will change the texture and taste of the biscuit.

Break down a recipe

Name: _____

Recipe
Break down the recipe and fill in the details below.

Main ingredients	
Flavourings	
Method	

Identifying hand equipment

Name: _____

Find out the name of each piece of equipment and suggest a use for it.

Name: _____

For each piece of equipment:
- Label the parts.
- List several appropriate uses.
- Identify safety considerations.

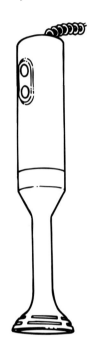

Name: _____

Accurately weighing and measuring ingredients is an important skill to learn. It is the secret of successful cooking. Chefs can estimate the amount of ingredients to use, but this is the result of years of practice and experience. To be successful in your cooking, careful weighing and measuring is essential. Modern food measures are given in grams and litres, but some recipes still use the old imperial measures of ounces and pints. Fill in this sheet and practise weighing and measuring in grams and litres.

Types of scales vary. There are balance scales and electric scales. It does not matter which you use as long as you check they are set correctly before you start.

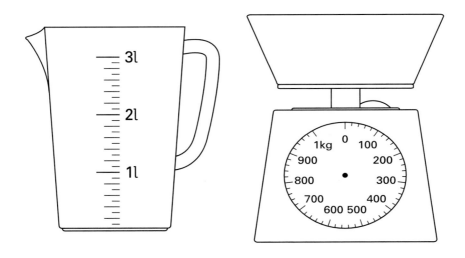

Item	Estimate	Real weight in grams	Score
1 large potato			
1 size-3 egg			
1 level tablespoon of flour			
1 level tablespoon of sugar			
1 large apple			

Extension Activity

1. Be a chef for a lesson and guess the weight of foods identified in this chart. Then check if you were right.
2. Complete Activity 15 on page 18 of the textbook – Keeping the right proportions.

Name: _____

Food Technology is a science. To create a successful food product it is important to understand how food is cooked by heat transfer. Read pages 14–15 in your textbook and, using the information about conduction, convection and radiation, describe how heat is transferred to cook the foods below.

Costing recipes

Name: _____

1. When you buy the ingredients for your recipe, keep the receipt and stick it to this sheet. Underline all the ingredients you use.
2. The price of each ingredient from the receipt can be misleading because you will not always use the whole packet of ingredients. You must use a calculator to work out the cost of the specific amount you use.

$$\frac{\text{Total cost of ingredient}}{\text{Total amount of ingredient bought (grams)}} \times \begin{array}{c}\text{Amount of ingredient}\\ \text{used (grams)}\end{array} = \begin{array}{c}\text{Cost of}\\ \text{ingredient used}\end{array}$$

3. Fill in this table.

Ingredient	Total amount bought	Total cost	Amount used	Cost of amount used

Total cost of dish: _____

Before giving a final total, it is important to consider the hidden costs of labour, time, energy (electricity and gas). This is not important when cooking at home for your family, but in industry it is a very important consideration.

Staple foods practical diary

Name:

As you make a variety of staple food recipes, record your observations about how staple foods are cooked and flavoured.

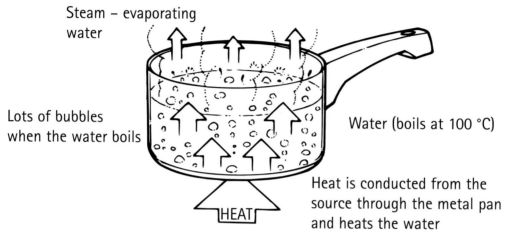

Steam – evaporating water

Lots of bubbles when the water boils

Water (boils at 100 °C)

HEAT

Heat is conducted from the source through the metal pan and heats the water

Record in this table how staple foods are cooked.

Pasta	Rice	Potatoes

Record in this table the flavours, ingredients and sauces you preferred.

Pasta	Rice	Potatoes

DESIGN in the Making © Pearson Education Limited 1999

Name: _____

Fill in the brainstorm diagram below to design a delicious staple food dish. If you have kept a 'Staple foods practical diary', use it to help you.

My preferred sauce
would be _____

My preferred staple food
would be _____

My recipe

To balance my meal I must
include a food that will
provide protein. I will use

_____

My preferred flavour
would be _____

Produce an ingredients list for your staple food recipe. Use pages 37–38 of your textbook 'Recipes for sauces' and modify one of them to suit your tastes. Create an original flavour by choosing from pages 30–33 of your textbook 'Adding flavour to food'.

My recipe is for _____ people	Ingredient	Weight required
Staple food (carbohydrate)		
Protein food		
Sauce		
Flavours		

Use your knowledge of weights and measures to help you fill in the 'Weight required' and then check with your teacher.

Extension activity
Draw a labelled and coloured diagram of your expected practical outcome. What will it look like and what dish will you serve it in? How will you make it appealing so that people will want to eat it?

DESIGN in the Making   © Pearson Education Limited 1999

Name: _____

Hygiene	Making	Temperature
Before cooking		Before cooking
		During cooking
		Test to see if the dish is thoroughly cooked
		Reheating instructions

Name:

Make a savoury light summer meal using pasta or a pizza base as an accompaniment.

You can choose between either of these two dishes and use the tables below to create a recipe of your own that you and your family can enjoy.

- Pasta with a sauce and flavourings.
- Pizza – choose your own toppings.

Pasta	Sauce	Flavourings
200 g dry pasta shapes *You must bring a medium casserole dish in which to take this home.*	**Cheese sauce** 1.5 pints of milk 2 tbsp cornflour 100 g cheese *or* **Tomato sauce** 1 tin of tomatoes 1 tbsp tomato purée 1 onion (optional) mixed herbs (optional) garlic (optional)	Meat – ham, bacon, tuna Vegetables – mushrooms, peppers, sweetcorn, spring onions, broccoli Or anything else you would like. Choose no more than three and think about combining the flavours.

Pizza base	Tomato sauce	Toppings
1 packet pizza base mix bought from the supermarket *You must bring a large tin in which to take this home.*	1 tin of tomatoes 1 tbsp tomato purée 1 onion (optional) mixed herbs (optional) garlic (optional)	Meat – pepperoni, ham, tuna, prawns, anchovies, chicken Vegetables – onions, sweetcorn, peppers, mushrooms, pineapple Cheese – mozzarella or cheddar cheese Make your own topping.

Garlic bread	Salad
1 French stick 1 clove of garlic 100 g butter or full-fat margarine	Create a colourful salad using lettuce, cucumber, tomatoes, spring onions, raw peppers. Do not use too many ingredients that take time to cut. It must be quick to make. *Bring a bowl in which to take this home.*

DESIGN in the Making © Pearson Education Limited 1999

Name: _____

Foods which have been prepared or processed to make cooking quicker and easier are known as convenience foods. A lot of convenience foods contain hidden fat, a lot of sugar, many additives, are highly salted, or contain large amounts of raising agents – and many other things which may not seem sensible to include in a healthy diet. On the whole, though, convenience foods:

- Are quick to prepare and therefore save time
- Are easy to store
- Save fuel when preparing and cooking
- Have little or no waste
- Offer a variety of unusual dishes.

In our modern, busy lives, most people consider these points as distinct advantages.

Complete the chart below with the names of a selection of foods.

Make a list of any disadvantages that you can think of, for convenience foods.

Frozen	Tinned	Dried	Freshly made (shop bought)	Bottled or in jars

Name: _____

How could you prepare the following meals using only convenience foods?

Shepherds pie	
Mixed vegetables	
Sponge puddings	
Ice cream	
Cod in parsley sauce	
Peas	
Chips	
Stewed apples	
Custard	
Curry and rice	
Apple crumble	
Cream	

Fill in the missing words

sensibly	pastry	foods	good	expensive	making

Convenience _____ can be included in a healthy diet, if used _____ . They can be _____ to buy if used at every meal. Items such as frozen puff _____ have many uses and the results are so _____ that it is hardly worth the long task of _____ them yourself.

Food likes and dislikes

Name:

Make a list of your food preferences. Try to explain why you like or do not like certain foods.

Foods I like to eat

Food	Why I like it

Foods I do not like to eat

Food	Why I do not like it

Diet profile

Name: _____

Name _____

Age _____

Height _____

Lifestyle _____

Favourite foods	Disliked foods

Food allergies

_____

_____

Diet preferences, e.g. vegetarian

_____

_____

Sporting activities

_____

_____

Opinion about healthy eating

_____

_____

Record the foods, snacks and drinks you eat for a meal, a day or a week using this chart.

Time	Red foods	Yellow foods	Green foods	Changes I could make

Red foods – High animal fat and sugar content. Low fibre. Fast foods.

Yellow foods – Low fat dairy, lean meat. Convenience foods.

Green foods – Fresh fruit and vegetables, staple foods, nuts, beans and pulses.

Name: _____

Food	Smell descriptor	Looks descriptor	Taste descriptor

Crumble evaluation

Name: _____

Draw and label a coloured diagram of your crumble.

Product evaluation

	Texture	Taste	Colour
Crumble			
Filling			

List the ingredients in your crumble as you would find them on a food package (i.e. most first, no quantities).

_____

_____

_____

Name: _____

Bacteria do not stop growing in cold temperatures! The rate at which they reproduce slows down, but in time food still spoils. Filling your fridge carefully and regularly cleaning it is an important part of keeping a kitchen hygienic.

After you have been shopping it is important to store food quickly and correctly. Put away this week's shopping carefully, placing the food in the correct sections of the fridge. Make a separate list of items that you would not store in the fridge.

This week's shopping
eggs, milk, cola, baked beans, bread, meat pie, frozen peas, joint of beef, trifle, bacon, lettuce, tomatoes, cucumber, cheese, yoghurt, butter, biscuits, pasta, tomato sauce, sugar, tea, coffee

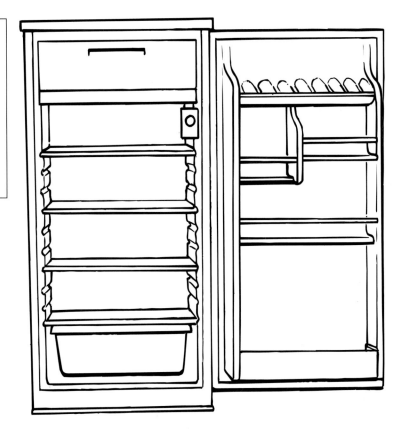

Extension activity

Refrigerators have been around for a long time and their basic design has not changed very much. There is a major problem with this design – raw meat should be stored at the very bottom but it cannot be because of the salad trays. Produce a modern design for a fridge that takes account of this fact.

Name: _____

Shop _____

Date _____

Product	Manufacturer	Packaging (e.g. loose, tinned, carton)	Method of preservation	Ingredients	Flavours

Design a snack food

Name: _____

Brief

Use your knowledge and skills from making soups, salads and milk drinks to design a balanced midday meal that is nutritious, healthy and safe to eat.

Before you begin, as a class research your favourite midday snack foods. You could carry out a shopping survey, research your school meals or keep a diet diary.

By the end of your research you should have discussed:

- The range of midday snack foods that are available.
- Whether or not they are healthy and safe to eat.
- Whether foods you make are healthier and safer to eat than those which you can buy.

Specification

Using the information you have gathered, and remembering your own dietary needs and taste preferences, produce a recipe design for your own home-made snack food. Your design must be:

- Healthy.
- Low in sugar but high in starch carbohydrate.
- Low in animal fat but high in protein.
- Able to be served hot or cold.
- Hygienically prepared and safe to eat.

Name: _____

Soup or salad

Basic ingredients to make soup:

- Water/Oil
- Protein foods – meat (e.g. cooked chicken), fish, vegetarian (e.g. beans or lentils).
- Starch carbohydrate foods – pasta, potatoes, rice.
- Vitamins and minerals – fresh vegetables, salad, fruit.
- Flavourings – salt, pepper, herbs, garlic, spices, stock cube.
- Extra protein, vitamins and fat – to enhance the flavour and texture (to thicken the soup) you can add cream, soured cream or yoghurt.

List the ingredients you will use to make your soup or salad.

_____

_____

_____

_____

_____

Name: _____

Bread Roll
Basic ingredients to make bread roll:
- Bought bread mix
  Decide on which type – brown, white.

The flour for the roll can be flavoured with herbs and spices, cheese, onion or sun-dried tomatoes, nuts and seeds. Or you can make a filling for your roll. This should be moist, for example garlic butter or cheese.

Milk Drink
Basic ingredients to make milk drink:
- Milk
  Decide which type of milk.

Decide how you will flavour the milk and increase the nutritional content.

List the ingredients you will use to make your bread roll or milk drink.

_____

_____

_____

_____

_____

If your soup or salad is low in fat or protein foods, then you need to include these in the bread or milk drink to balance the snack.

Name: _____

Answer the following questions in complete sentences.

1. List the main ingredients in your food product.

   _____

2. State which ingredients provide which nutrients.

   _____

3. Use the dietary analysis to assess how nutritious your product is.

   _____

4. If you consider your product not to be healthy, how could you modify the recipe to make it more healthy?

   _____

5. Was your product easy to carry and eat?

   _____

6. Are the ingredients easily purchased? Are they available throughout the year?

   _____

7. What was the cost of your product?

   _____

8. Do the ingredients require storage; for example, refrigeration?

   _____

9. Which cooking methods were used to prepare the product; for example, creaming, kneading, folding, baking, whisking?

   _____

10. List any electrical equipment you used and explain why you decided to use it. Was it the right decision?

    _____

11. How long did your product take to make?

    _____

12. Were any convenience foods used? If so, why did you use them?

    _____

13. What other food products would you suggest to eat with your product?

    _____

14. What is the size of your product? Measure the length, width and weight.

    _____

15. Could a package be made to fit your product? If so, how?

    _____

Name:	

This is a professional case study, therefore the language used should be formal and precise. Try to present a logical and coherent piece of work that clearly demonstrates your understanding of an industrial process.

Suggested project outline

Introduction
- Outline the purpose of this report.
- Outline the timescale for this project.

Contents page (Do this last)

Research – market research
Shopping survey to identify a gap in the market for a 'new biscuit'.
- Aim – explain what is the purpose of the research.
- Methodology – explain how you conducted the research.
- Results table – graphs etc.
- Conclusion – identify a gap in the biscuit market.

Recipe design
Your biscuit must be original in some way, i.e. shape, flavour, colour, texture.
- Explain the basic ingredients needed to make biscuits.
- Explain how to make biscuits.

- Explain how you are going to improve the biscuit.
- Refer to the conclusion in your research.
- Recipe trials – write up, in detail, all your practical sessions.
- Taste test – write up, in detail, all your taste testing sessions.
- Evaluate all the biscuits you made.

Recipe modification
Explain how you would need to modify your recipe to mass produce the biscuit successfully.

Detailed costing for all outgoing expenditure

HACCP – production plan

Packaging design
- Produce sketches and drawings of your proposed packaging design.
- Suggest appropriate material to preserve and protect the biscuits.
- Produce sketches of your label.
- Produce a nutritional label.

Photograph of the prototype

Recommendations
- Report conclusions and recommendations to supermarkets.
- Sell your biscuit to a possible buyer.

Recipe specification

Quantity	Ingredients	Special considerations
100 g	Self-raising flour	To bind the mixture together To give a light airy texture to the biscuit
75 g	Margarine	At room temperature To add moisture to the mixture To give flavour
50 g	Caster sugar	To give a sweet flavour to the mixture To give a crunchy texture

Name: _____

Domestic production and manufacturing batch production

A safe and hygienic environment is essential in an industrial environment. It is optional in a domestic kitchen. Laws are in place to ensure high standards of hygiene are implemented and environmental health officers are one of the many bodies of people that enforce the law.

The main controlling systems used in the food industry are:
- Food Safety Act 1990
- The Food Safety (temperature control) Regulations 1995
- HACCP (Hazard Analysis Critical Control Points)

HACCP was introduced by the Pilsbury company and NASA in the 1960s to make sure that astronauts had food that was safe to eat when they were in space. The system has been adopted by the food industry to ensure the safe manufacture of food.

The aim is to identify and control all hazards and risks associated with any stage of the food production before the manufacturing of the food begins. It is not an afterthought but part of the design process. A hazard is defined as anything in the food production system that may result in harm to the person eating the food. The hazard may be Biological (bacteria), Chemical (e.g. detergent left in the food), or Physical (a foreign body, e.g. blue plaster). A Critical Control Point is a point at which it is essential to remove the hazard to get rid of the risk.

HACCP helps to establish a quality assurance programme. Critical Control Point helps to establish a quality control process that reduces waste.

Setting up a production line

Five important issues need to be discussed when designing the production process.
- Quality assurance
- Personal hygiene issues
- Health and safety
- Portion control or product size
- Identification of and action to eliminate faulty products before packaging.

Quality control

Quality control is a system that inspects and tests a sample of the items at different stages whilst they are being made, and records the results and comments for analysis. Quality control procedures predict failure before it happens.

Quality assurance

Quality assurance is the overall approach which ensures high standards of quality throughout a company. It includes the development and monitoring of standards and procedures, documentation and communication.

Manufacturing a quality product that is safe to eat does not just happen. It is carefully planned for and conscientiously managed.

Name: _____

This shows the design and make process in food technology. You start with a problem that needs an edible solution. This loop shows the way to approach the problem and find an appropriate and high-quality solution.

Task
You have been asked to make items for sale at the School Christmas Bazaar refreshment stall.

What do you need to know?
What do you need to think about?
Type of food required
Size of items
Eat with one hand
Reasonably priced
Attractive
Healthy
Resources available
Cost
Time available
Equipment
Storing and packing options.

Evaluation
Does the finished item do the job you set out to do?
Is there anything that you should have found out or planned to do, but didn't?
Did you get the costing right?
What did you think of the finished result?
What did customers think?

Practical implementation
Make the product.

Collecting information
Recipes
Costings
Maintaining quality
Oven temperatures used.

Planning
Variety of items
Ingredients required
Oven use.

Research brainstorm

Name: _____

To find an appropriate solution, you should research the problem thoroughly. There are many sources of information available. Brainstorm which are appropriate to your needs. The diagram below will provide a starting point.

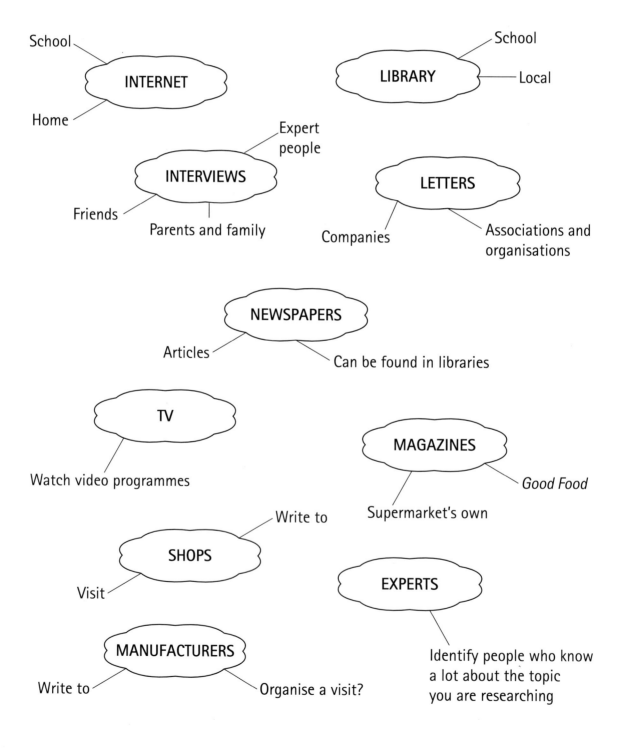

Name: _____

What are you researching? _____
_____

Describe the product that you are researching in detail.

_____

_____

_____

_____

Identify possible sources of relevant information and how you will present your research findings. When you have collected the information, tick in the boxes to show whether what you gathered was useful.

Source of information	Useful	Not useful	How you will present the findings

Sample letter for requesting information W36

Name: _____

Use this sample letter as a guide if you are writing to ask for information to help your research.

When writing your letter:
- Make sure it is polite
- Check your spelling
- Keep it clear and easy to read
- Keep it short but say exactly what you want.

Address the letter to a particular person or post holder so the company knows to whom the letter should be passed.

Use the school address so the letter is more official, or use school headed paper.

Food Technology Department
My School
DT1

The Production Manager
ABC Food Retail
My Road
Towcester TO1

Dear Sir/Madam,

I am a Year 9 student undertaking a food technology project.

I should be most grateful if you would send me information about the manufacture of your food products.

Thank you for any help which you are able to provide. I enclose a stamped addressed envelope.

Yours faithfully,

Peter Smith

This is to confirm that this student is engaged upon a school project. Any assistance would be very much appreciated.

_____ Teacher

Say who you are and indicate why you want information.

Be specific and say precisely what information you would like.

End by saying 'thank you' and that you are enclosing an SAE.

Sign the letter clearly or type your name under the signature.

Have your teacher endorse the letter to increase your chances of a reply.

DESIGN in the Making © Pearson Education Limited 1999

Name: _____

Product – what are you designing and making?

_____

_____

_____

_____

Audience – who are you designing and making your food product for?

_____

_____

_____

_____

Purpose or function – why are you designing and making it?

_____

_____

_____

_____

Risk assessment – where do you need to be careful?

_____

_____

_____

_____

Cost – refer to the price of a similar product on sale at a supermarket.

_____

_____

_____

_____

Remember – Quality and Hygiene. Your product must be attractive
and appetising as well as edible and safe to eat.

Food product specification

Name: _____

Use the following headings when you write a specification for your food product.

Function
What is the purpose of your food product and whose needs is it suitable for?

Ingredients
Identify the main properties of the ingredients and how they will be used to achieve a specific taste, texture or finish to your product.

Health and Nutrition
Identify specific health or diet related considerations and state whether your product will be low fat, low sugar or high fibre.

Portion Size
Define the size and estimated weight of your product. State how many people it will serve.

Visual Appeal
State the shape, colour and any decorative features you will use to make your product appetising and appealing.

Product Consistency and Texture
Describe the desired consistency of certain aspects of the product during making (e.g. sauce thickness or biscuit dough consistency) and also the desired texture when your product is complete and ready to eat.

Method of Preservation
Describe how you will preserve your product.

Expected Shelf Life
Suggest a possible 'waiting' time before your product must be eaten.

Method of Testing
Describe how you will test to ensure the quality of your product is achieved and maintained.

Quality
Describe ways and methods of ensuring the quality of your product is maintained and an accurate, consistent result is achievable more than once.

Name: _____

Giving reasons why your solution is appropriate is very important.
Here are some ideas to help you.

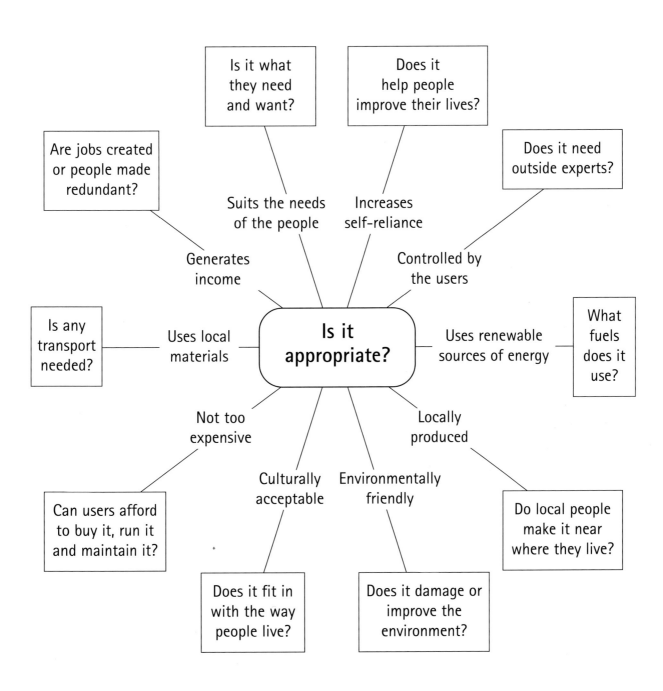

Name:

There are many important issues to consider before you can begin making. Here are some examples.

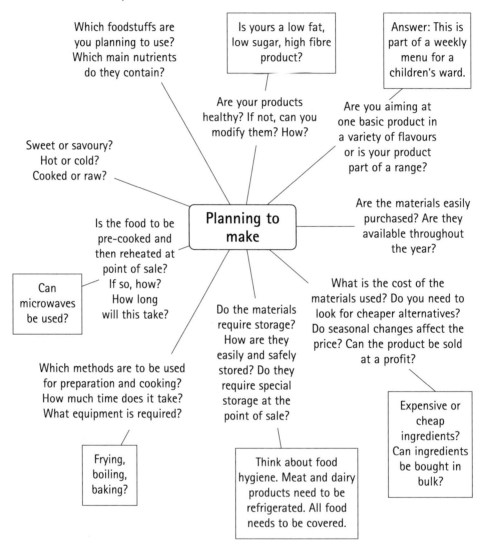

General points to think about
1. The special nutritional needs of the person or people.
2. Time of year and time of day.
3. Variety in flavour, texture, colour and appearance.
4. Family meal or special occasion?
5. Money available.
6. Time to prepare.
7. Variety of cooking methods – top of cooker or oven? Think of the cost of different cooking methods.
8. Shopping – buying food in season.
9. Ability of the cook.
10. Likes and dislikes of the person or people.

DESIGN in the Making © Pearson Education Limited 1999

Name: _____

If you modify a recipe, use this sheet to record the changes.

Ingredient	Change to	Reason for change

New ingredients list

Weight/quantity	Ingredient

Changes to method

Original method	Changes

Nutritional analysis

Name: _____

Find out the nutritional value of your meal.

Ingredient	Amount used	Energy (k joule)		Protein		Fat		Carbohydrate		Fibre	
		Actual	Per 100 g	Actual	Per 100 g	Actual	Per 100 g	Actual	Per 100 g	Actual	Per 100 g
Totals:											

Was the meal healthy and balanced? _____

Fill in the nutritional information for labelling the package.

Average values	Per 100 g	Per portion
Energy		
Protein		
Fat (of which saturates)		
Carbohydrate (of which sugars)		
Fibre		

Extension activity
You could make your own label to include more detailed information, such as vitamins and minerals.

Name: _____

Time	Making activity	Specialist knowledge

Name:	

Describe your intentions and what you hoped to achieve with your product.

_____

_____

_____

_____

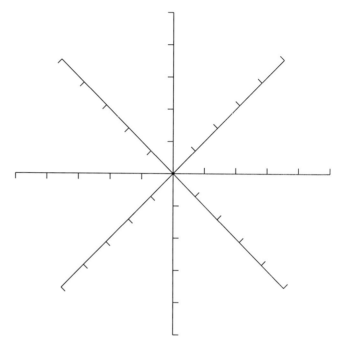

Using the sensory descriptors from the textbook and any others you consider to be essential to the success of your product, fill out the star diagram right.

Rate your success

Using the information on the star diagram, your observations and other people's opinions of your product, fill in the chart and rate your success.

Think – was your product:	Yes	No
A distorted shape		
Poor in appearance		
A poor combination of ingredients producing an undesirable taste		
The wrong combination of ingredients producing an undesirable texture		
Over-cooked		
Under-cooked		

Lots of 'Yes' means you need to improve your product.

Lots of 'No' means your product is successful.

Evaluation against specification

W45

Name: _____

Specification	Achieved	Not achieved	Comments	Modifications	Possible solutions
Function – was your outcome fit and suitable for its intended purpose					
Ingredients					
Health and nutrition					
Portion size					
Visual appeal					
Product consistency and texture					
Product taste					
Hygiene considerations					
Method of preservation					
Expected shelf life					
Method of testing					
Quality control measures					

Name: _____

Describe the quality and success of the design

_____

_____

_____

_____

_____

Suggest improvements

_____

_____

_____

_____

_____

Test results or opinions from experts

_____

_____

_____

_____

_____

Have you successfully communicated with your target audience?

_____

_____

_____

_____

_____

Self evaluation

Name: _____

Look at the product you have made and taste it. Write down what you think about it.

During this lesson I made _____

The good things about my product are:

Looks _____

Taste _____

Smell _____

I could have improved my work by

_____

_____

When I was doing my work I had the

following problems: _____

_____

I solved these problems by

_____

_____

_____

_____

_____

The new skills I have learnt are

_____

If I make this product again I would change:

Looks _____

Taste _____

Smell _____

Did you do the following?

	Yes	No
Safety		
Put away stool, bag and coat?	___	___
Use oven or hob safely with oven gloves?	___	___
Put apron on?	___	___
Hygiene		
Use clean tea towels and dish cloths?	___	___
Clean hands and nails?	___	___
Tie hair back and take rings off?	___	___
Organisation		
Keep a tidy work surface?	___	___
Follow instructions on recipe sheet?	___	___
Timing		
Arrive at lesson on time?	___	___
Complete work on time?	___	___

Oven temperatures

Name: _____

Temperature	Type of dish	Electric	Gas
Cool	meringues	150 °C	2
Very moderate	large rich fruit cakes, milk puddings, egg custards	170 °C	3
Moderate	biscuits, small rich buns, victoria sandwiches	180 °C	4
Moderate	casseroles	190 °C	5
Hot	roasted meats, baked fish	200 °C	6
Hot	shortcrust pastry, scones, batters, flaky pastry	220 °C	7
Very hot	whisked mixtures, bread	230 °C	8

Name: _____

NUTRITION INFORMATION

Typical Values	PER 100g (3.5oz)	PER BISCUIT		PER 100g (3.5oz)	PER BISCUIT
ENERGY	1911 kJ	147 kJ	FAT	15.4g	1.2g
	454 k.cal	35 k.cal	of which SATURATES	6.5g	0.5g
PROTEIN	7.5g	0.6g	MONO-UNSATURATES	6.5g	0.6g
CARBOHYDRATE	71.4g	5.5g	POLYUNSATURATES	1.7g	0.2g
of which SUGARS	20.6g	1.6g	FIBRE	2.3g	0.2g
STARCH	49.5g	4.7g	SODIUM	0.5g	Less than 0.1g

PER BISCUIT	35 CALORIES	1.2g FAT

INGREDIENTS

WHEATFLOUR, SUGAR, VEGETABLE AND PARTIALLY HYDROGENATED VEGETABLE OIL, MALT EXTRACT, SALT, RAISING AGENTS: SODIUM HYDROGEN CARBONATE, AMMONIUM HYDROGEN CARBONATE, DISODIUM DIPHOSPHATE; GLUCOSE SYRUP.

* CONTAINS MILK AND SOYA

CH TEA

INGREDIENTS

WHEATFLOUR, SUGAR, VEGETABLE AND HYDROGENATED VEGETABLE OIL, WHOLE MILK POWDER, PARTIALLY INVERTED REFINERS SYRUP, DEXTROSE, RAISING AGENTS: SODIUM BICARBONATE, AMMONIUM BICARBONATE, DISODIUM DIHYDROGEN DIPHOSPHATE; SALT, CAROB BEAN FLOUR, EMULSIFIER: SOYA LECITHIN; ARTIFICIAL FLAVOURINGS, COLOUR: BETA-CAROTENE.

06 FEB

NUTRITION INFORMATION

TYPICAL VALUES	PER 100g (3.5oz)	PER BISCUIT	TYPICAL VALUES	PER 100g (3.5oz)	PER BISCUIT
ENERGY	2158 kJ	308 kJ	FAT	27.0g	3.8g
	516 k.cal	74 k.cal	of which SATURATES	16.6g	2.3g
PROTEIN	5.3g	0.7g	MONO-UNSATURATES	6.5g	0.9g
CARBOHYDRATE	62.9g	9.0g	POLYUNSATURATES	1.5g	0.2g
of which SUGARS	38.5g	5.5g	FIBRE	1.0g	Less than 0.1g
STARCH	24.3g	3.4g	SODIUM	0.4g	Less than 0.1g

INGREDIENTS

WHEAT FLOUR, SUGAR, VEGETABLE OIL AND HYDROGENATED VEGETABLE OIL, ANIMAL FAT, PARTIALLY INVERTED SUGAR SYRUP, MOLASSES, CULTURED SKIMMED MILK, RAISING AGENTS (SODIUM BICARBONATE, AMMONIUM BICARBONATE), SALT, GINGER EXTRACT, LEMON OIL.

NUTRITION INFORMATION

	AVERAGE VALUES	
	Per 100g	Per Biscuit
ENERGY	1981kJ	198kJ
	471kcal	47kcal
PROTEIN	5.6 g	0.6 g
CARBOHYDRATE	75.0 g	7.5 g
of which sugars	32.0 g	3.2 g
FAT	16.5 g	1.7 g
of which saturates	7.4 g	0.7 g
FIBRE	1.7 g	0.2 g
SODIUM	0.5 g	0.1 g

Name: